# CHILDREN'S POETRY BOOK

Jenny South

**MINERVA PRESS**
WASHINGTON LONDON MONTREUX

**Children's Poetry Book**
Copyright © Jenny South  1995

ISBN  1  85863  328  1

First published 1995 by

MINERVA PRESS
10 Cromwell Place
London SW7 2JN

Printed in Great Britain by
B.W.D. Printers Ltd., Northolt, Middlesex.

# CHILDREN'S POETRY BOOK

To Tim, Sarah and Emily

# MUD

Soft and squelchy
Brown and thick.
Buckets full of chocolate sauce
Or sticky treacle.


It sticks to your hands,
It seeps into your hair,
And squashes between your toes.
And it's not like sand;
That's fine and fun.
It's wet and soggy,
Hides in your ears,
Creeps up your nose,
And covers your clothes.


It makes your Mum mad
'Cos the garden's a mess.
The buckets you've used,
And the spades no less;
But worst of all are your clothes and hair,
And your body is covered
Layer upon layer...
With dried-up mud
That won't come off,
Except with a scrub,
And a long hot wash,

That'll turn the bath brown
And make certain you're clean...
But the grime round the rim
Shows the fun there has been!

# CHRISTMAS EVE AND THE BAD DOG

It was quiet...
The presents were wrapped...
Christmas lights shone brightly in the
dark room...
The dog was sleeping, or was she
waiting
Till we went out of the door...

WHEN WE GOT BACK THERE WERE
        SWEETS ON THE FLOOR,
Wet chocolate wrappers which the dog
had chewed
And bits of soap which she thought was
food.

She hadn't used scissors,
Thought her teeth would do,
And she did want to chew
Through that sticky caramelised Mars
bar.

But all we saw when we got back
Was Christmas wrapping,
And a dog - flat on her back;
Snoring soundly and dreaming
Of a sweet soapy Christmas.

# ST NICK AND THE BRICK

St Nick's a bit thick.
He doesn't fit
Down chimneys.
He moves too quick;
Hits his head on a brick.
But don't take the mick
Of little old Nick!
He does the impossible.
Rides the skies on a sleigh,
Goes round the world in a single day.
He brings each child a present or two;
And the sleigh bells ring out -
Happy Christmas to you.

# IS BLACK BURNT OR BEAUTIFUL?

Burnt toast.  Black...
Burnt onions are crunchy and oily.
Black spaghetti is hard and crusty.
Worms have black on the tips of their
bodies,
And they move slimily in the wet soil.
But cats are black and soft
With beautiful green eyes.
Black can be beautiful
But it can be burnt -
And Black.

# A WORM IS...

Slithery
  Slimy
    Squiggly
      Wriggly
        Squirmingly
          Segmentally Fat.


Oh!  I do wish that worm
Would disappear beneath the ground
Without a sound
Where he cannot be found.
But then I might poke him
With a rake or a spade.
Splice him or
Slice him;
Make holes in his belly.
But he'll jerk away
Like a frightened old jelly.


That's enough of gardening.
I'll leave the worm and the spade.
His fat little belly.
I'll get some rest now...
And watch the cartoons on the telly.

# PUDDLES

Puddles are
Like mirrors
That you look in,
Jump in,
Splash in;
And kick the puddle away
To cover others
In rain water.
Puddles are fun
Because YOU
Look back at YOU,
And clouds.
And the mirror moves;
So it changes what you can see
Momentarily.
But it's sad
When the sun
Has come;
Like a magician
With his wand and fun,
To vanish the puddle
Into his Box of Tricks...
Did the sun have his hat on?

# WOLF! WOLF!

I cried "wolf" but the wolf didn't come.
I thought I would be naughty and have a
bit of fun.
I said I saw a monster walking down the
street.
The monster was my mother on her own
two feet!

I said I had no money when really I had
some,
The man was going to shoot me when
he had no gun!
I kept crying "wolf", but the wolf didn't
come.
I kept being naughty and having lots of
fun.

I said I'd had no dinner, nor hardly any
tea,
My face was full of smiles and my mind
was full of glee.
I said I had the chicken pox, and so I'd
go to bed,
That way I wouldn't go to school, I'd stay
at home instead.

I kept crying "wolf" but people walked away,
They would not listen to what I had to say.
There's a monster, there's a giant,
There's a spider on the floor.
Why won't they listen? I'm calling "wolf" for sure!


I know it isn't true, "wolf" is what I said,
They'll be no "wolves" tomorrow; only "BEARS" instead!

# POP, BANG AND WHIZZ

Lemonade, pop, fizz and burp,
Out of the can it bubbles and slurps,
Down your mouth and into your throat,
Sometimes you splutter, sometimes you
choke.


Often the drinks come out of the can
With a spill and spray and a very loud
bang.
The fizz and the bubbles cascade to the
floor,
Leaving you little to drink for sure.


Sometimes the top of the can gets stuck,
And then it seems you're out of luck.
For no matter how hard you try to
succeed
You just cannot get the drink you need.


The bubbles and burps come into your
throat,
They make you laugh, they make you
choke.
You burp just like a half-crazed frog
Or an open-mouthed demented dog.

So remember the bubbles, the burps and
the fizzes,
So think of the bang and the pop that
whizzes,
Showers and spurts on your hands and
your head,
Leaving you wet and sticky and red!

# BIRDS AND SLINGS

Throngs of birds
That move and dart
From tree to tree.
It would be fun
To make a sling
From twig and twine
To hit a bird
With feathers fine.
But birds can fly
And children can't.
Slings can break
And birds can dart
To hide behind the nearest tree.
I bet you can't hit me; hit me!
But boys get bored and need their tea.
And as for me,
I'll have the last laugh...


You can't catch me!  You can't catch me!

# CONKER MADNESS

Autumn and conkers
It's time for fun.
Horse-Chestnut time
Has just begun.
The coloured leaves
Lie dank and wet
Beneath the tree,
Their fingers stretched  -
Reflecting coloured rainbow light,
Glistening droplets sparkling bright.
Conker shells and leaves arrayed,
And shiny fruit that is displayed.
So let us have a game or two
With our conkers bright and new.
I'll try to smash yours, that's for sure!
But never mind we'll find some more.
The conkers think it's fun to play
And hide from us this Autumn day.
I'll shake more fruit down from the tree,
But sadly they won't fall for me.
The wind will blow them down instead.
Ouch!  It's raining conkers on my head...


Oh well, let's go and find another tree.

# SQUASHED HEDGEHOGS

Hedgehogs are prickly -
I don't think they're tickly.
They scurry along looking this way and
that;
But sadly we see that they sometimes go
splat.
They don't look where they're going,
They cross busy roads.
Well why can't we do it,
We've seen all the toads!
The trouble is hedgehogs aren't all in
their prime,
They just can't cross quickly to make it in
time.

Hedgehogs look lovely.
I'm sure they are cuddly.
They have sweet little noses
That go sniffing for bread.
It's hard to imagine them dead
And squashed flat.
Their bits on the road;
It's a pity that!

In memory of hedgehogs
I think of the night,
The saucer of milk
His fur in the light.
I remember him shuffling across the
grass;
Waiting for my steps to pass.
But I'll always remember the prickly ball,
And wonder whether he was a hedgehog
at all.


PS. I wonder if I really could tickle him!

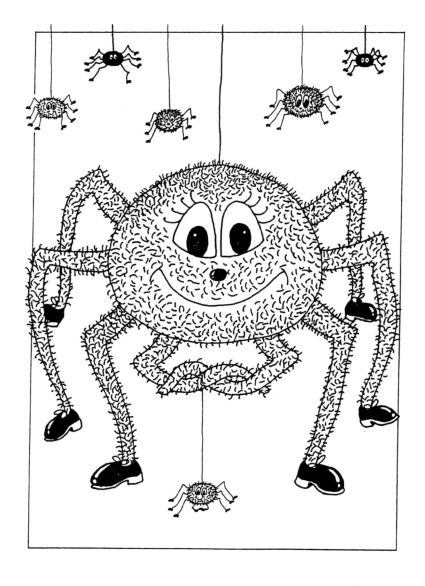

# MY BLACK HAIRY SPIDER

My spider is creepy.
It is bulgy and black.
And it also is fat.
My spider is hairy and happy
With luminous green eyes
That chase you after dark.
But never in the light...

# TICKLES GALORE

I hate to be tickled.
I'd rather be pickled
Than suffer the laughs,
My legs in the air,
Like a sprawling giraffe.


Whatever you do, don't tickle my feet,
For then I will roll around on my seat;
And end up careering around on the
floor,
I just can't stand it anymore!
I wriggle along the ground like a worm
Flat on my belly, with a funny old squirm.
The giggles just get worse and worse.
I think that I am going to burst
Forth with a squeal and a smile on my
face,
I just don't think I'll stand the pace.
So don't tickle me under the chin
Or I shall look mad as a cat with a grin.
My body keeps writhing, I'm in such a
trance.
Please will you give me another chance!
My head is reeling, it's in a flat spin.


So!  Don't you ever tickle me again!

# HALLOWEEN BALLOON BALL

Balloons that pop and hop and dance,
Balloons that bounce and jump or
prance,
Balloons that burst, balloons that float,
Balloons that sail away like boats
Into the air with a doh-si-doh,
One, two, three and away they go,
Not too fast and not too slow;
Around the room with a hop, hop, hop,
Down they fall with a pop, pop, pop.


Red ones, yellow ones, blue and green
Take your partners, it's Halloween.
Spin or twirl around the room,
Up in the air and into the gloom
Dance and fly with witches' brooms.
Float above the pumpkin lights
Past witches' cats and out of sight.

# LADDERS THAT CLIMB INTO THE SKY

I like ladders
That don't wobble
And are high.
But best of all
I like the ones
That stretch up
into the sky;
And the top is hiding
In the clouds.


The cloud world
Is more fun
Than the ground.
The ground world is in our eyes
But the sky world is in our minds.


I can see strands of pink tissue
That lead to princess castles.
Gardens of white flowers
In soft blue grasses
Giving colour and light
To the dream world of the sky.


The sky world is yellow and happy,
But the ground world can be sad.
My world is both worlds.

# LOLLIPOPS

I love lollipops!
That are icy
And taste nicey.
I like hard ones
That don't melt
Too quickly.
Soft lollies
Break off round your mouth
And are messy.
The bits fall on your shoes,
And your pleasure
melts,
Like the ice-cream
That fell on the floor,
Or the juicy raspberry one
That got away.

# FEAR IN THE NIGHT

Strange shadows dance
On my bedroom wall.
They move when the wind moves
Or car headlights shine in through my
curtain.
But sometimes the shadows move with
no wind.
Then I feel strange and creepy.
The shadows make weird shapes
And become monsters ready for my
world of dreams.
The monsters merge into
A darkening room.
Fear is everywhere,
But not under my bedclothes.
It lurks in silence under my bed.
The shadows are silent and scary.


I am alone in the black
And without light.

# A PAINT BOX

God has painted beautiful colours in the
sky
With a giant-sized paintbrush.
His brush is covered in rainwater.
He uses the sunlight for the colours,
And prefers to use his own box of paints.
Oil paints or pastels are no use to him.
He wants a wet look,
So he uses the rain and the sun for his
picture.

# THE DECK CHAIR SPIDER

Black and hairy
Or hairless;
Legs that move
Quicker than you do;
Spiders that stroll round your bath,
Or spiral from the ceiling
Like they're on a high wire
At the circus.
Or, they hide in a corner,
or in a crack -
Sprint towards you
From a hole in a wall
Or from a secret place.
Sometimes they jump into your lap,
You scream and cry;
They die.
They tuck their legs in -
Just like you would fold up
A deck chair.

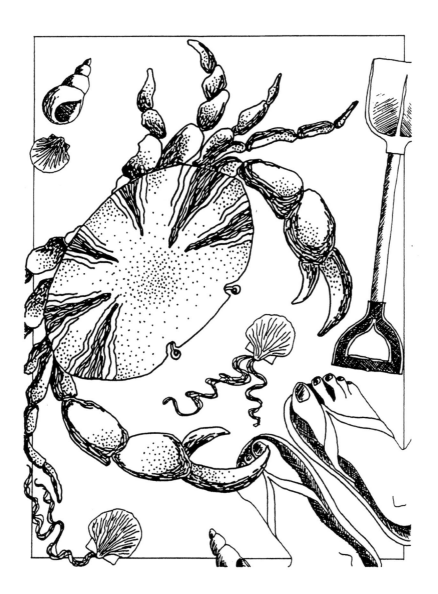

# THE SEA AND FUN

Crabs and Claws
That might touch you
or bite you,
Or disappear in soggy sand.
The claws could pinch my toes
If my feet got stuck.
Worm patterns
Trailing along the beach
When the tide ran
Far away and into the haze.
Cool breeze by the sea
Playing games with the waves.
Catch me if you can!
You can't splash me!
Footprints and pools,
Gritty sand like it had
Been baked in a hot oven.
I can hide things in the sand,
And make streams
That come from the sea.
I can feel
Stony sand clinging to
My salty body
And refusing to dry.
Ice-creams that stick
And lollies that
Drip onto you
In the hot summer sun.

# SHADOWS AT NIGHT

They lurk behind cupboards
And under the bed.
They stand there in silence,
I'm so full of dread.
Sometimes they're like saucers,
Sometimes they are long,
They might stand alone
Or as one of a throng.
But they've one thing in common,
They wait till it's night,
And creep round the room
In the half-baked light.
They don't have a face,
Just an eerie black shape -
They hang from the ceiling
And over you drape.
They scream in silence in your ear,
And then like magic they disappear.


There are shadows galore
In the light of the day,
And I don't mind them anyway.
But at night when I'm under my duvet
cover,
They stand there and hover -
And creep
Into my
Dream Time.

# FISH FACE

Fat face
Freckle face
Fish face
Four eyes
Spotty
Big nose.
Metal mouth
Big ears
Noddy
Goofy
Thick head
Hairy
Or
Hairless
Nutty
As a fruitcake
Dummy or Dumbo
Skinny ribs
I think you're crazy as a clown;
Or mad as a hatter,
So there!

# FACES EVERYWHERE

There are faces on the curtain,
There are faces on the wall.
Faces on the ceiling
And out there in the hall,
The faces they are gruesome.
The faces can be mad,
The faces can just peer at you.
Some look so strange, some sad.
Sometimes you cannot see them,
But just then they appear.
And just when you have seen one
It quickly disappears.


Sometimes the faces come at you
From lots of odd directions.
Their eyes just seem to glare and stare,
And fix you in your bed,
That when you glance right back at some
You're lying there in dread.
Eventually the faces fade,
You can't see where they are.
But for sure you know
They've not gone very far...


Tomorrow they'll be back!!

# SECRET PLACES

I can hide down drains,
Or in dark dank tunnels;
Go where no-one has been before.
I can hide inside tree trunks
Or in long grass;
Or caves in a hill or a cliff.
I can hide in bushes
Or in dusty cupboards;
That smell of old mothballs.


I can hide anywhere
That I cannot be found.
Up in the air
Or down on the ground.
The best bit of hiding
Is being under cover
Where you'll never be found;
Not even by your old muvver,
Who'll never discover
The secrets you're keeping,
When you're awake or while you are
sleeping.
For the places YOU hide in
Nobody goes.
No-one will discover,
No-one will know.

# SECRET PASSAGEWAYS IN OLD HOUSES

Passageways that lead
Behind rooms,
And you can hide there
In secret and in the quiet.
You can talk but
No-one can hear you.
You can disappear from one room
And appear in another
Through panels in walls.
Old houses can have secret rooms,
And secret staircases.


But can you find them?

# A MARBLE OLYMPICS

Glass eyes rolling on a bumpy pavement
Or along the cracks of a floor,
Big eyes or little eyes
Colliding,
Cloudy eyes, running along
Without legs
Chasing one another.
A marble Olympics
Of fun and colour,
Running and rolling,
Jumping and throwing,
Twisting and turning.
Circus colours,
Clowning around
A marble arena.
A disordered procession
Of wayward marbles
At the Marble Games.

# HIDE N' SEEK

I hide -
You seek.
You count - and
Don't peep.
Count to 10 -
No looking.
I'm ready -
So steady -
Then go.
Come find me
If you can  -
Bet you can't.
Keep looking -
Everywhere.
In the hall,
Up the stairs.
Give up?
There you are!
You're not allowed
In there!
Cheating?
That's not fair!

# DREAMING

Floating,
Flying,
Breathing,
Dying,
Soaring,
Winging,
Flapping,
Singing,
Sailing,
Gliding,
Hovering,
Riding,
Circling,
Swooping,
Winding,
Looping,
Into the air and
Dancing with the light.
Climbing to the clouds,
Whispering in the wind,
And reaching for the sun.

# SING A SONG OF YO-YOS

Yo-yos go up, yo-yos go down,
Up in the sky, down on the ground.
Yo-yos can be yellow, yo-yos can be red;
Yo-yos can reach the floor or your head.
Yo-yos can reach out, yo-yos can reach in.
Yo-yos can curl up or stretch out very thin.
Yo-yos can be little, yo-yos can be tall -
Long as a snake or small as a ball.
Yo-yos can roll or jump up and down,
Swing and lift, over and round;
High as the ceiling, low as the floor,
The yo-yos have stopped,
Now there are yo-yos no more.


My yo-yo keeps jerking,
I think it's not working.


My yo-yo's got stuck; just my luck.
Oh well! I'd better go and buy another yo-yo.

# TALKING TREES AND TELEPHONES

Magical trees
Magical minds.
Trees that talk
In night and day time.
Whispering gently
In case you should hear
The secrets they keep
In seasons and years.
Voices are raised
As the wind spins around,
Circling the tree-trunks
And over the ground.
The insects hide
As the words rush by -
Into the branches
And up to the sky.


To a faraway time
And a faraway place,
Scattering the words
In the darkness of space.
So the trees will whisper
Or talk or sing.
They might say a word
Or not breathe a thing.
They may howl or cry,
They may talk or moan,

But one thing's for certain
They don't use a phone...
Why use a phone??
When the wind whistles by -
Carrying their words
To the faraway sky.

# ROPES

Thin as string,
Fat as a pig,
Big
As a whale.
Short as a stick,
Thick
As a rhino.
Wide as a wall,
Small
As a mouse.
Tall
As a hill,
Still
As a stone.
Long
As a line,
Fine
As a hair,
Rough
As a road.
Tough as a boat,
And twisty like stairs.
Ropes of all types,
Ropes everywhere...

Ropes for skipping, ropes for heaving,
Ropes for fishing, ropes for weaving.
Ropes for pulling, ropes for dyeing,
Ropes for knotting, ropes for tying.
Ropes for tugging, ropes for boats,
Ropes for buoys to keep afloat.
Regalia of Ropes, or a
Ropey Regalia.

# CREEPY CRAWLIES

Creepy crawlies
Can have hundreds of legs.
They dash round the floor
Or climb into your bed.
They move so fast you can't be sure
If they're under the table or by the door.
If they are red, or if they are black,
Or whether they're down in that tiny
crack.

..................................

Sometimes they go marching out of the
hall,
If only they'd vanish down by the wall.

..................................

The creepy crawlies attack your toes,
They seem to follow wherever you go.
The ants may be little, the spiders big,
The cockroaches, fleas and the earwig.
Fleas like your blood, lice like your hair,
The bloodsucker sucks, but the ants
don't care.
Bees will sting you, the mosquito will
bite;
Millipedes, centipedes, what a sight.

...................................

Millions of insects, hundreds to find,
Long-leggedy beasties of every kind.
Creepy crawlies, you can never be sure
Whether they'll go out, or knock at -
Your FRONT DOOR...

# HOP SCOTCH

One to ten
Count again.
Throw a stone in a square,
Over there.
Don't miss,
Just jump.
Mind the line,
That's number nine.
Hurry up,
Now quick, jump!
You've thrown the stone to number ten
OK - begin again.
The stone is now in number one,
All right, so have some fun.
Hop into the second square;
Don't cheat, just be fair.
I'll get the stone to number three,
So please avert your gaze from me.
I've hopped right into number eight,
But can't you see
The line's not straight.
The chalk has smudged,
I can't be sure -
Was that square for number four?
Had enough?  Let's have some tea.
We'll come out later.
You and me.

# CLOUD CLIMBING

Clouds are for climbing.
Clouds are like seas
To sail away on
Above the breeze.
Giants in the clouds,
Castles in the air.
Ladders that reach up high
Into the shadows of the cloudy sky.


Clouds are like pillows
To sleep on, to play.
Clouds can be climbed up
In darkness and day.
Clouds are for children
To sit on, to stand,
In thrones and palaces,
In faraway lands.


Clouds can be big, clouds can be small,
But the ladders you'll need have to be
tall,
They need to be bendy and stretch up
high
To reach the clouds in that far-off sky.

The Cloud land is different,
Not like earth at all.
There aren't any gates or fences or
walls,
No limits to what you can do or say;
The Cloud land is magic but it's faraway.

# A SEA OF BOTTLES

Green bottles, brown bottles, clear
bottles blue -
A bonanza of bottles, enough for me and
you.
Little bottles, thin bottles, wide bottles
tall,
Rows of glass bottles at a market stall.
So -
Pick a glass bottle, write a note or two  -
Saying how are you or how do you do!
Throw it in the sea, send it far away,
To India or China or even Mandalay.


One day when you are very old (you
might be 84),
The postman will come knocking at your
own front door.
Another message, in a bottle, from a far
off place and time,
Takes you back to childhood and when
you were just nine.

# NOISES IN THE NIGHT

There's an eerie scream in the depth of
the night,
And a silence of terror before the light.
Outside your window are murmurs or
moans,
Or was it a gasp or a growl or a groan?
Was it a screech, a hoot or a howl?
Or a scream, a squawk or even a yowl?


The noises at night need not be so loud.
They can be silent and soft, and quiet as
a cloud.
The whispering walls can leave you in
dread.
The squeaks and creaks can lurk under
your bed.
And creepy shadows dance round the
room
Leaving you frozen with fear in the
gloom.

The creaks that you heard on the stairs
last night
Disappear in the morning light.
The gasp and the growl, the screech and
the scream
Vanish away like a nightmare or dream.
The birds that sing in the sky at dawn
Turns the terror of night to a new day
born.

# CLAMBERING

Clambering over the sea-weedy rocks
That dip down to the sea,
Clambering up the highest hill
To see what I can see.
Skidding down the grassy slope
To climb back to the top,
Clambering up the limestone caves,
But eventually you stop.
You clamber up the gnarled trees
That twist at every turn,
Until you slip and fall below
Into a clump of ferns.
You'll climb the wall, you'll climb the
fence,
The tree-house and the tree,
Until you want your eggs and chips,
And now it's time for tea!

# SCHOOL DINNERS

I hate fresh fruit and salty peas,
Only soggy chips for me.
Spinach, gristle, grease and stew?
Only sausages will do.
Don't give me boiled potatoes,
Runner beans or peas.
Only crisps and hamburgers,
No semolina please.
All the milky puddings, they make me
feel quite sick,
So I'd prefer to leave them or don them
down quite quick.
Remember I don't want my health, only
lots of pleasure.
I'd rather eat the chips and crisps, and
repent then at my leisure!

# NETS AND SLIME

Let's go fishing and find all the grime
Lurking at the bottom as well as all the
slime.
We could find some broken bottles, and
tin cans too,
The oil is very thick and slick and the
fishes few.


My net is full of mud and oil and little bits
and pieces,
Who knows what we'll find here, maybe
little mices.
The weed is very smelly, the oil is wet
and slick -
The silt that's at the the bottom is very
brown and thick.


What else is in the water? I hardly dare
to think!
All I know for sure is that there is a rotten
stink.
The smell of rotting rubbish is in the
watery sludge,
The waters will not move and the cans
refuse to budge.

I wish instead the pond was clear, not all
of this pollution.
It's really not a problem, there is a quick
solution.
Take your broken bottles, and your
rubbish right away;
Why spoil the countryside and my lovely
fishing day?
All I wanted was to fish, not find the
grease and grime.
Perhaps weed and water will be there...
The next time.

# SOUNDS OF THE SNOW

Musical bells sing in the snow,
Peeling away to the valley below.
The singing voices beckon as
Footsteps crunch on the snowy ground,
And snowflake silence is all around.


A cowbell stirs in the icy night,
Children singing with lanterns bright,
Laughter and voices fill fire-lit rooms -
Inviting you in from the cold and the
snow,
To Christmas magic and a fireside glow.

# PICK A SAUSAGE

Sausages fat, sausages small,
Sausages many or not at all,
Sausages fat, sausages thin,
Sausages with very thick skin.
Sausages red, sausages brown,
Sausages lean, sausages round,
Sausage that sizzles,
Or fat that will fizzle
Inside the pan and onto your plate.
Sausage you'll love or sausage you'll
hate.
Sausage for dinner, sausage for tea,
Sausage for you, sausage for me.
Sausages old, sausages new,
Sausages hundreds, sausages few,
Sausage with herbs, sausage with
flavour,
Lots to sample and to savour.
Sausage with eggs, sausage with peas,
Sausages with chips, sausage with
cheese.
Sausages plain, sausage on sticks.
Now it's time for YOU to pick.

# WHICH BEAR WILL YOU CHOOSE?

Polar bears are hairy,
But they look a bit scary.
They are big and bright
And sparkling white
Like brushes in the snow.


Koalas look lovely,
But they're not all that cuddly.
They sleep still as stones
But they are never alone,
In the Eucalyptus trees.


Grizzly bears will stare;
Surprise you and glare.
They will peer and ponder,
And disappear yonder
Into the dark forest.


Teddies become worn,
They are often torn,
They grow old,
But they are like gold,
And you love them forever.

# THE MAGIC OF SHELLS

Shells hide secrets that you do not know.
They'll hide in the sand, or below
The waterline or in hidden caves,
Or lie quite still in sandy graves.
They'll cling to rocks and secrets keep
Until the tide creeps, over them
And they swim away into the ocean.


Shells hold secrets that you'll never
know.
Creatures hide in little holes
In the shell, where they cannot be seen,
And where once they might have been.
Creatures use shells for their homes and
their rest;
But we are never sure where they are or
what they look like.


The colours of shells is a mystery to me.
Did they come from the deepest parts of
the sea?
From pebbles or rocks along the shore,
From rainbows or sunlight? We don't
know for sure.
Could the wind in the shells be the
waves from the sea?
Shells they are magic, and lovely to me.

# NIGHT MAGIC

The night is black,
The stars are white,
The houses lie still
In the quiet moonlight.
A cat creeps along
An old brick wall,
There's a rustle of leaves,
And a faraway call
Of a distant owl.
There's wind in the trees
And a lonely howl
Of a dog in the dark.


The night is cold,
The moon is bright.
There's mist in the air
And the frost is white.
A hedgehog scuttles,
His feet in the ice.
There's a crisp sound of footsteps,
And the squeaking of mice
In a frozen barn.
There are lights from the windows,
People in the warmth
And flickering fire-light.

# ANIMAL GYMNASTICS

Tortoises will trudge through the
undergrowth,
At the speed of a sloth.
A flea will spring as high as a dog,
Leaping up high like a warty frog.
A kangaroo will jump up high
But not as high as a bird in the sky.
A fish will swim in a greeny sea,
But will he swim faster than me?
A mouse will scurry into his hole.
A horse will trot and also the foal.
Calves cavort and cows will walk.
Monkeys and parrots and birds just talk.
The cheetah runs, the snake he slinks.
The spider climbs and the skunk - he
stinks.
Jumping, flying, walking too.
I'll do them all as well as you.

# HORSES AND HOOVES

Hundreds of horses, so many hooves.
Wind in their tails, they're all on the
move.
Cantering crazily past hedges and trees.
Knees and legs and manes in the
breeze.
The turf is upturned as they thunder by -
A blur of motion against the sky.
Panting through nostrils, fear in their
eyes,
They want to escape, so they gallop and
fly.
The horses are wild, they want to be
free,
They speed along towards the sea.
For the sea is big and the sea is wide,
There's a place for horses to live and to
hide.
The horses need freedom to roam
through the land,
They don't want the stables, or owners,
or man.
For they long to be wild, they yearn to be
free.
They need the expanse and the blue of
the sea.

# THE TEDDY SCHOOL

Teddy bears furry, teddy bears knit.
Teddies of straw or cloth kits.
Royal bears or children's toys,
Bears for all the girls and boys.


Fabric, patchworks fur or in rags,
Teddies with hats or carrying bags.
Some look moth-eaten, some in tatters,
Bears can be quiet, and some like to
chatter.


Bears full of happiness, bears full of
tears,
Bears to last for years and years.
Broken ears and eyes that are blind,
Teddies of all sorts and all kinds.


Arms and legs that need repair,
Attention they need, and love and care,
Victorian bears that have grown old too.
Lots of teddies, the shabby or new.

Bears can be characters, some may be
bad.
All bears are loveable, some may look
sad.
Teddies alone, or teddies together,
BEARS, I will love you for ever and ever.

# EYES

Eyes alive, eyes dead,
Eyes left, eyes right,
Eyes green, eyes bright,
Eyes old, eyes new,
Eyes many, eyes few,
Eyes that move, eyes alert,
Eyes aloof, eyes hurt,
Eyes that love, eyes that care,
Searching eyes, everywhere.
Eyes for anger, eyes for joy.
Eyes for crying, eyes annoy,
Eyes for talking, eyes for blinking,
Eyes for silence, eyes for thinking,
Eyes are mirrors, windows, too,
Eyes that look from me to you.

# ALICE THE CAT

My cat is covered in blotches and
stripes,
He has splashes of brown and splodges
of white.
Sometimes he is ginger, sometimes he is
red -
He's covered in paint from his tail to his
head.

His nose is jet black, his tail is all fluffy,
His fur is long, he's matted and scruffy.
His eyes are cloudy, blue and white,
His paws and his claws, oh what a sight!

My cat's name is Alice, he's a hairy
heap.
I can use his tail to mop or sweep.
He's used as blotting paper when the
water's on the floor.
There is no other cat that would give you
any more!

But I like it best when he purrs on my
lap,
Or sprawls himself out by the fire on a
mat.
His whiskers displayed, and his legs in
the air,
His tail and his fur straggling
everywhere.

# TALKING TREES

Each tree has a face etched on its bark
When it is day-time and when it is dark.
Branches are hair that waves to and fro,
Blown by the wind and the rain and the
snow.
The eyes and the nose and the mouth
can be seen
In woodland surrounded by carpets of
green.

Spring flowers adorn the forest floor,
The scent of bluebells the trees can be
sure.
They hear the rustle of leaves in
September,
Cast their minds back and then they
remember -
The insects and animals preparing for
rest,
Autumn migration, when birds flee their
nests.

Trees seem to talk with the wind    whistling by -
  Beneath a cold and cloudy sky.
  Children touch trees to see how they feel,
  The bark can be rough and the tree is real.
  They like to climb right to the top
  And from a height the fruit they drop.


  Trees may be quiet, trees may be still.
  But they can be loud when the wind is shrill.
  They can shriek in pain when they're cut down,
  Lie still as a stone upon the ground.
  Trees whisper gently when the wind softly blows,
  They have a language we don't really know.

# BALLS

Balls go hopping
Bouncing and running.
Balls in the air,
On the field,
Keep on coming
Towards you.
Over you,
With a skip and a jump.
Behind you,
Over you,
They land with a bump.
They bruise your head.
They bang your nose,
Hit your knee,
Or land on your toes.
Skim over the grass,
Fly into the air,
You wouldn't know
The ball had been there
Until your eye
Turns purple and black.
There are stars in the air
And a thud:
And a crack!
Ouch!

# NIGHT EYES

Eyes that are green
And peep -
And creatures creep.


In the dark
Yellow eyes
That stare
And glare
Filling you with fear -
At night.


Eyes in the trees
Eyes on the ground
Eyes with no sound
Twinkling and blinking
Like lights
Going on and off -
In the bedroom.

# FOR FUN AND LAUGHTER

# NELLY'S POT BELLY

There's old Nelly
With her big pot belly,
It sticks out in front
Like a big fat lump
Of a baby or a ball.
It's only flab and all.
As she walks her belly bobbles.
The tummy wobbles
Up and down, left to right
Without a sound.
Her skirt splits,
Revealing it.
She tries to hide
Her inside;
Begins to topple
And her belly flopples
Onto the floor.
You want to know more.
She's plenty of flab
And a mouth to match.
She jibs and jabs -
"Oh help me fight my flab,
My flab is drab!"


So think of Nelly
With her big pot belly.
She quakes and shakes
Like a red currant jelly.

# HAIRY HARRY

Harry was a caveman.
You would say he was a heap.
You cannot see his skin for hair.
He's a fat and hairy creep.
His beard is very curly,
And it is turning grey.
The growth that is upon his chest
Is like a load of hay.


For hairy Harry has fair skin
And so his hair is yellow.
He is big and very bulgy,
This funny caveman fellow.
The hair upon his head sticks up
Like it was dry cut grass,
Waiting for the mower,
But harvest-time went past.


His hair is really dirty
It's full of lice and fleas.
If only he would wash it
And get the dirt out please!!
So GO and wash your awful hair
And keep clean-shaven too.
For then you will smell fresh and sweet,
Not like stale fish and stew.

# MIRROR MAGIC

Mirrors at the fairground.
Mirrors happy, mirrors sad.
Magic in the mirrors,
Mirror monsters, mirror mad.
Mirrors, they are nonsense,
Mirrors give distortion,
Mirrors change your body shape
Out of all proportion.
The mirror shows your tummy fat,
Your legs are short, now fancy that!
Your head may grow to twice its size.
Your ears stick out, your hair will rise.


Mirrors show a weird reflection.
Of arms and legs; a strange collection.
So can the bits the mirror sees
Really show it's you or me?

# INK BLOTS

Ink blots,
Dots and dashes,
Splodges and sprays,
Spots and splashes,
Splatters the desk,
Flicks onto the floor.
Bespeckled with blotches
And yes there is more...
So the
Freckles and spots,
The dots and the blots
Cover your nose,
Your eyes and your ears.
You're sprinkled with fun
And your face disappears.
ABRACADABRA!
Who put the lights out?

# NOSES

Noses are for
Blowing,
Smelling,
Scenting,
Breathing,
Sniffing,
Whiffing,
Niffing,
Wiping,
Streaming,
Blocking,
Running,
Kissing,
Rubbing,
And saying HELLO!

Noses are for
Colds,
Handkerchiefs
Tissues,
Snot,
And sneezing,
Nubbing
And snubbing.

Noses are
Big,
Small,
Fat,
Freckled,
Elongated,
Aquiline,
Roman,
Square,
Holey,
Rotting,
Hairy,
Spotted
And smelly.

# CLOWNS AND FLOWERS

Clowns are daft.
They make you laugh.
They look like giraffes
If they're walking on stilts.
They have colour and craze,
Madness and fun.
A bonanza of balls
And backward hats.
Trousers that don't fit
And hang below
Bottoms with braces.
Elephantine shoes
That slip and trip
Over wet bananas.
Weeds growing in
Clowns hats.
Water sprays.
Showers
And flowers in
Circus Summers.

# GHOSTLY CAPERS

Ghostly shapes
Drape
And gape
Over you.
Ghostly ghouls
And white capers
Chase you
In laughter,
Breathing and sighing,
Rising, floating,
Flying, Dying.
Whispering eerily
Shadowy shapily,
Gapily;
In mist and vapour.
Ghostly capers
Scarily, airily,
Wearily, jeeringly
Leeringly, fearingly.
Frighteningly, brightly,
Sparkly, darkly,
Deathly,
Drabingly, grabingly
Shiver and quiver
In Quaking Land.

# THE OLD LADY AND THE MOUSE

The old lady yelled, "There's a mouse by
the chair!"
She screeched and screamed but
nobody cared.
There's a rat on the carpet, there's a rat
on the floor;
The old woman shouted, "Help me, Help
me!" more.


Her hair stood on end; she jumped up
and down.
The little brown mouse thought she was
a clown.
He thought it was a kitchen, NOT a
circus tent;
The old lady seemed a trifle bit bent.


She had some silly spectacles perched
upon her nose,
She wore a tight skirt and funny old
clothes.
This can't be a woman on a trampoline -
All she seemed to do was to jump and
to scream.

I'll come back to-morrow, then I'll eat the cheese.    Please don't shout at me, I only meant to tease.

# THE OLD MAN'S HEAD

The old man's head looks a bit bent,
And where it's bald there are lots of
dents.
There are bits of hair trying to grow,
And hide the balding patches you know.
There are moles and freckles on top of
his head,
And the smell up his nose is like stale
bread.
For this man doesn't wash nor keep
himself clean,
And you just do not know where he has
been!
There's hair on his body, hair on his
neck,
But the balding patch shows not a speck
Of hair or whiskers or follicles too.
The old man is bald, what about you?

# LADY LA DI DAH

Lady La Di Dah has a hat with bananas.
The flowers on her hat look like her
pyjamas.
She's aristocratic; her hair is dyed red
To match the robin on top of her head.
Her voice is posh with a hat to match,
The straw sticks out like a wayward
thatch.
The net hangs down to hide her face,
Frills and fripperies and la di dah lace.
Her nose is upturned and her hat held
high,
The parrot squawking against the sky.
Her eyes steer a glance, she cuts a mad
dash,
The fruit and the flowers and the birds
they flash
Of colours so bright, so vivid and gaudy.
Her hat and her hair and her face is just
tawdry.
La Di Dah Lady your frills must go,
Along with the feathers and parrots and
show.

# BARE NECESSITIES

Are you a bear or are you bare?
If you're a bear
You'll have brown hair,
Over your body and down to your toes,
That's the way a brown bear goes.
If you're a polar, then you'll be white,
Looking like soap powder, shiny and
bright.

Bears don't wear jumpers or skirts or
vests,
Only their coat and their fur is the best.
They don't need pyjamas or knickers or
clothes,
Bare necessities, only bears know.

People are different, they need to be
covered.
They want to wear woollies and scarves
and be smothered.
They like to wear jackets of fur and
leather,
To keep themselves dry whatever the
weather.
To cover their bodies, to cover their skin,
To keep the warmth and the heat right in.
They hide under clothes, heaven knows
why!
Bears don't do it, so why you and I?

# YAKATY YAK, YAKATY YAK

Yaks are hairy
Squarey
Layery
Starey
Beary
Glarey,
And like a fairy
Elephant.


Yaks are yakaty
Crackety
Maggoty
Haggaty
Raggety,
Staggaty
Baggety
Flaggety
And Naggetty
Like an old sheep
In the snow.

# THE BANANA BOYS

Nutty is the yellow one, though he's not a
nut,
He's thick skinned and he's greedy, he's
a fat and ready glut.
Skinny's like a sausage, except that he is
yellah!
I think that if you saw him you would love
this crazy fellah!


Custard you may slip on if he's lying on
the floor,
He's carefree and he's lazy as I'm sure
you've heard before.
Freddy is the one who often is quite sick;
He's green and very pallid - we'd best
call the doctor quick.


Blotchy is the squashy one that monkeys
love to eat;
Or, if they step on him he just oozes on
your feet.
Stinky is the one which has gone all
runny,
He's smelly and he's mouldy; he thinks
it's very funny.

Banana boys are fun, they play all sorts of games.
I'm sure you must have heard -
It's the Banana Hall of Fame!

# JAWS AND CLAWS

Crabs have claws.
Sharks have jaws.
Pincers are for clawing.
Teeth are for gnawing
Through bones and skin.
They both like flesh
But leave a mess
Of bits and pieces.
Torn skin
When the pincers are in.
Ripped limb,
And a sharks fin
Zig zagging in the sea.
The crab and claws,
The shark and jaws with
Bobbing bits of me
Scattered in a reddy sea.

# A BOX OF NOSES ALLSORTS

Hippos' noses
Have two tiny holes.
Horses' noses
Are pink and soft
With long whiskers.
Parrots are posers
With pin pricks
For their noses.
Pigs have snouts
For sniffing and whiffing.
Dragons puff steam
And scream
With laughter and fire.
Beaver noses are
In wet hair
With water and swimming.


Bison and bear noses are
In wild America.
Noses are high
In the giraffe sky.
Bat noses are
In black caves
And blind black.
Wet noses are
On dogs out walking.
Rabbits' noses

Twitch
And run
In the hot summer sun.
Near noses
And faraway noses.
Noses can be noisy
And quiet
In snoring and sleeping.

# TOFFEE APPLES

Toffee apple on a stick,
I'm biting it.
Brown and shiny sticky balls
I love you all.
The apple pulp,
The toffee brittle,
I like you if
You're big or little.
The inside part is very chewy,
The shiny ball is brown and gooey.
Apple sticky,
Apple licky,
You're soft and munchy,
Brown and crunchy.

Toffee apple you are yummy,
Especially when inside my tummy.
Toffee sugar, toffee sweet,
In my mouth you're such a treat.
Toffee apples, toffee craze;
I'm in the sticky sugar phase -
Of stuffing toffee down my throat,
Spluttering, I start to choke.
The toffee bits give me holes,
So to the dentist I must goes,
The drill comes out. I HATE the pain,
But I'd eat you ALL again.

PS. Three cheers for toffee apples.

# MICE, CHEESE AND CHAIRS

Mice like cheese; ladies like chairs.
Mice on the floor take ladies unawares.
Mice like to squeak
And ladies love to shriek.
So,
Ladies touch the ceiling,
Mice touch the floor.
Ladies grip their chairs.
Mice like to gnaw.


Ladies in paralysis,
Mice frolic round.
Ladies stiff as boards.
Mice on the ground.
So,
Mice have the last laugh,
The ladies die with fright.
What a silly spectacle
And NOT a pretty sight!!

# GYPSY ROSE LEE

I DON'T BELIEVE the Crystal Ball.
Fifteen children, tell me more.
They'll have big eyes and pointed *noses*
Have no hair and won't wear *clothes*
They'll wake at night
And sleep by day.
Fight and tousle;
Won't work just play.
You'll live a long time
In trouble and strife -
Like the woman in a shoe
Leading a DOG'S LIFE!!!

# BEARINESS

Hairiness
Beariness
Scariness
Lairiness
Stariness
Luriness
Cuddliness
Muddlyness
Snow white bears
On ice
Grizzlies
In Wild Woods
Swimming bears
Climbing bears
Walking bears
Honey bears
Funny bears
Story bears
Gnawy bears
Teddy bears
Picnic bears
In the woods today.

# MEAT SALAD

It's lurking in the lettuce,
It is brown and it has legs.
It is very long and hairy
And I'm not sure if it's dead.


Could it be that it is meat?
I've not had this before.
It doesn't look that tasty,
I really am not sure.


I do not see it hiding
And it will come to grief,
When you bite into its legs
And the tasty lettuce leaf.


So if you see one moving
And if it's on your plate,
Don't attempt to eat it,
You might just have to wait.


I know you have an appetite
And can't wait for your dinner.
But if you can't resist the food
You could get so much thinner.

You'll end up feeling queasy
And then be sick and faint.
The insect in the lettuce
Looks like meat but AIN'T.

# THE FLEA CIRCUS

Roll up, roll up for the Circus Show,
Fleas on the high wire,
To and fro.
They leap on a rope,
They jump up high,
Loud applause to reach the sky.
Fleas on horse-back round the ring.
Circus clowns
They joke and sing,
Jumping up on lions' heads.
"Didn't they do well?" they said.
Juggling balls and acrobats,
Down they topple
Onto their backs.
Spring through hoops,
Slip down slides
Onto the cycles,
Off they ride.
Glamour fleas on top of ponies,
Circus nonsense, loads of baloney.
Ring master flea comes out to bow.
So fleas, you take the ring right now!

# DUSTBIN DICK

Dustbin Dick nicked rubbish from bins,
Got put inside for all of his sins.
He took apple cores and bits of tuck,
I'll tell you soon how he ran out of luck.


His favourite food was banana skins,
These he'd find at the bottom of the bins.
He liked crisp packets and old fags too,
He ate old potatoes but he didn't mind
new.


One October night when the sun had
gone down,
Dustbin Dick was fingering around.
He found some fish and chips inside the
bin,
He stuffed himself crazy, he was so very
thin.


The very next dustbin he reached for
some pop
"Hello! Hello! This will have to stop."
(Policeman)
Dustbin Dick swung right around.
"Now tell me quickly what it is you've
found.

I see you have a drink in your hand just there
But money in the other, so how do you dare?
I think you'd better come with me down to the station,
I need to have a word with you and get some information.
Loitering for mouldy food or with what intent
Stealing lots of money to pay for the rent."
But Dustbin Dick thought a bag he had taken
The policeman said he knew he was mistaken.


Dustbin Dick was locked up in  a cell,
He won't be nicking rubbish for quite a spell.
How the money got there we'll never ever know,
Dustbin Dick was innocent, except the food he stole.


Do you think he was guilty?

# WORMS CAN...

WORMS CAN...

Jiggle
Wriggle
Twiggle
Squiggle.


WORMS CAN BE...

Pickled
Tickled
Lickled
Prickled
Sickled


WORMS MAY BE...

Spliced
Sliced
Diced
Liced

Eaten
Beaten
Meaten
Sweeten

WORMS ARE...

Squelchy   Slimy
Belchy    Grimy


WORMS NEVER...

Wear Wellies
Have beer bellies
Are smelly
Or watch the telly

## CHEWY GUM

Chewing gum sticks.
You find it everywhere.
Under the table,
Stuck to your chair.
The worst bit is
If it's in your hair,
People will stare
At the chewing gum there.
It's like elastic
Not hard like plastic.
It's pink or white -
An ugly sight.
If it's on your bottom
It leaves a stain.
Oh what a pain!


Chewing gum's tasty, but
It looks a bit pasty
After you've sucked it
For over an hour.
It looks like paste
Or watery flour.
Your jaws start to ache,
As if eating gristle,
Or a large sponge cake,
The flavour has gone.
It's time the gum went

Into your stomach,
Or down an air vent.
So don't leave it wasting
On a table or chair
It will stick to a bottom
Or somebody's hair!

# JUDE IN THE NUDE

Dear Old Jude would sit in the nude
Even on a cold day.
His friends came along
And said it was wrong,
But they refused to play.


So Dear Old Jude couldn't see it was
rude
Not to put any clothes on.
He was left all alone
To sit on his own,
But he still couldn't see it was wrong.


So Jude in the Nude couldn't see it was
rude
But decided he would get dressed.
So his friends would play
Whatever the day
And said to wear clothes was best.

# CUSTARD PIES

Custard pies get in your eyes,
They may get in your ear.
They sit upon a plate and then...
Your face will disappear.
You're caked in yellow custard,
You're eyes just cannot see
The face of your opponent
And the people full of glee.
You're covered in bright yellow,
And sticky custard muck.
Why did you stand and take it?
Did you not think to duck?
Now you pay the dreadful price
Of smelling of pie odour,
Dripping blobs onto your feet
Of sticky ice-cream soda.


So next time there's a party
Of hurling custard pies,
Make sure it's you that has one,
So THEY get the surprise.

# FLUFFY CLOUDS ON STICKS

Candy Floss
And sticky bits.
Sugar clouds
On fairground sticks.
These clouds are very sticky,
Not like the ones up high.
They stick upon your nose and lips
Like icy sorbet pie.


The clouds on sticks get in your hair,
The clouds up high they float;
Candy floss is pink and fun
Not like a pink sky boat.

# BUBBLY GUM

Bubbly blow
Bubbly gum
Bubbles so pink
Bubbles have fun.
Bubbly blow,
Bubbly burst
Bubbles so big
Bubbly first.


My bubbly is bigger!
Your bubbly is small!
My bubbly's the winner!
Yours not at all!!
My bubbly will burst
With a very large pop.
Your bubbly has holes in,
So...
Your one's a flop!!

# ANIMAL CARNIVAL

Photograph Daft
Laugh.
Joking Jackasses
Hairy hyenas and
Humour.
Rumour of
Kookaburra crazy
In the old Gum Tree.
Tee Hee.
Dance of the Flea.
Fly in the sky
Whizzing by
Dogs' noses.
A tailless cat
A wart covered frog,
A bee's dance of eight,
And a hairless dog.


Racoons wearing masks
Creeping round bins,
Nosing to see
If the food is in.
Bats hanging from ceilings asleep
And dreaming of flying.
Shampoo and set
For prim little poodles.
Afghans' coats looking like

Tangled Spaghetti.
But don't try eating it.
Grandad goats.
Old beards trailing the fields.
Cows jumping madly.
Calves cavorting.
The Animal Carnival Craze!

# DUSTBIN DIRTY

| | |
|---|---|
| Sticky | Sicky |
| Mucky | Yukky |
| Dark | Dank |
| Slimy | Grimy |
| | |
| Banana Skins | Bin |
| Orange Peel | Feel |
| Dead Mice | Lice |
| Old Kettle | Metal |
| Black Shoe | New |
| Green pea | See |
| Hair Gel | Smell |
| Stale Cheese | Fleas |
| Meat Pie | Fly |
| Fish Bone | Alone |
| Grey Plug | Bug |

Dustbin Dirty, dustbin black.
It's dark inside the dustbin
It's wet and very grimy.
If you put your hand straight in,
You'll pull out something slimy.

# APES

You look at him and be looks back too.
Could it be that he is you?
You both have eyes and ears and noses,
Except that he does not wear clothes.


Could it be that you were he
A long time back in history?
You would have had hair on your body or
breasts,
And over your legs or your big broad
chest.


You stare at him and he glares back at
you.
And you wonder *who* is looking at *who*.
Looking at apes through the mirrored
glass,
But looking at You in the long ago past.

# ANTS

Ants in your pants.
Ants in your bed.
Climbing ants
Up your leg.
Ants go walkabout
Round the table
Or the chair.
They go after jam
If the jam is there.
Ants go crawling
By the drainpipe
Or the wall.
They'll walk in the kitchen
Or down through the hall.
Ants will find the syrup
They'll find the sugar too.
They don't care where -
In the bedroom or the loo!
Ants in boiling water,
Ants that swim away.
Ants in the poison
Ants in the spray.
So red ants, black ants,
Killer ants too.
You may have stamped on one ant,
Your may have sunk two,
But you always can be certain,
They'll come back for YOU!!!

# PEOPLE SHAPES

You could be
Lanky
Lolloping
Tall
Thin
Fat
Featured
Straight
Short.


You could have
Spindly legs
Knobbly knees
Broad buttocks.
Feet displayed
Like a penguin that
Waddles Wobbily.


You might have
A Walking Stick back
Be stiff and staggery.
Have a Camel hump.

In the black you might see
Shapeless shadows
Or stick insect people.
*Painting shapes
in the shadows
Or in the sun.

---

* LS Lowry (Famous Painter)

# WIGGLES AND ALL THAT!

Bottoms wiggle.
Ears jiggle.
Teeth chatter.
Voices natter.
Legs are long.
Noses pong.
Breasts bobble
Tummies wobble.
Backs are arched.
Mouths are parched.
Feet stink
Skin is pink.
So people
Wiggle
Jiggle
Chatter
Natter
Are Long
Pong
Bobble
Wobble
Are Arched
Parched.
So
Wiggles to you!

# NUTTY OR NUTS FOR YOU

Coconuts, Cashews,
Ready to eat, ready to cook.
Hazel nuts, almonds,
Come and look.
Brazils and chestnuts
At Christmas time;
Some are for your friends,
Some are for mine.


Cashews are like moons
That hang in the sky,
Walnuts are clusters of stars
Floating high.
Peanuts in plenty
With salt from the sea
Nuts for you
And nuts for me.


So don't be insulting and call someone
nuts!
A nut is not stupid or hairy or mad.
A nut is for pleasure,
Makes you happy, and glad.

# A NOSE SELECTION BOX

Toffee noses stuck up
In a box.
Noses with soft centres
Caramelised or runny.
Hard brown noses
Roll up roll up
And select your nose.
Green ones, yellow ones
Lemon or Lime
Nutty noses,
Iced or minty.
Nice noses to eat,
Come and buy, come and buy.
All the way from the factory to shop.
Supplies for the
Nosey Selection Box.

# NOSEY OESY

Put your whole nose in,
Put your whole nose out,
In out, in out, shake it all about.
You do the nosey oesy
And you turn around,
That's what it's all about.

Chorus: Oh! the nosey oesy,
Oh! the nosey oesy,
That's what it's all about.

Put the little noses in,
Put the little noses out,
In out, in out, shake it all about,
You do the nosey oesy
And you turn around
That's what it's all about.

Chorus: Put the big noses in,
Put the big noses out,
In out, in out
Nose it all about,
You do the nosey oesy,
And you turn around,
That's what it's all about!

Chorus: Nosey Oesy!!

# A PLETHORA OF NOSES

Noses can be spotted
Or warty or moley,
Blotchy or speckled
With freckles.
They can be white as
A Ghost,
Red as a red Indian,
Or brown as chocolate.
They can be sunburnt and blistered;
Scaly, or
Pale as the moon on a
Cold night.
Noses make brilliant
Ski slopes and can look like
Camel humps.
Noses are pointed,
Long,
Squiggly
Triangular.
They can be
Hot or cold,
Sticky, sweaty,
Sloppy.
You can rub noses,
Kiss noses, love noses.
They are for clowns,
Wizards, Witches,
And People.
Noses are nonsense,
And they are for everyone.

# A PARROT PRISON

PRETTY POLLY[1]
Pretty Dolly[2]
COLOURED BIRD
Lovely Girl
BEAK FEATURES
Freak Creature
TWIT YOU
Whit Who... (Wolf Whistle)
FEATHERED CLOWN
Get 'em Down.
EYES BRIGHT
What a Sight
BIRD OF PREY
Go Away
FOOD TONIGHT
Good Night.

---

[1] Large Capitals denote the person talking to the Parrot
[2] Small letters denote the speech of the Parrot

# THE POX

I've caught the Pox, the dreaded Pox,
I'm covered all in blotches.
They're in my nose, behind my ear
In lots of little notches.
They creep into the crevices and tiny
little cracks -
Between my toes, around my lips,
And up my arms and back.

If you start with freckles, and then you
add the spots,
You would not know you had some skin,
Just brown and red ink blots.
You hide your body in the bed,
In case someone should see
You looking like a crazed giraffe
Or a spotted chimpanzee.

The spots they start to itch,
And you scratch them all to scabs.
They leave you looking like a fish
With scales on top of flab.
The Pox, the Pox, the Chicken Pox,
Or could it be just spots.
Like Spotty of the Bash Street Kids.
Or maybe they are not.

"You've got the Chicken Pox, so there!"

# FEET

Feet can be wrinkled
Look cracked and crinkled.
The skin can be scaly
And dry as a bone;
Can be sprinkled with powder
Smell of clam chowder.
The corns and the calluses
Can be splattered with cream.
Toenails can be sharp,
Stick out in the dark
Be laden with grime
And stink of cream cheese.
Feet can be wet
Be covered in sweat,
The space in the toes
Is caked with dirt.

So keep your feet hiding
Where the warts won't be seen,
Where the scum and the smells
Can be hidden from view,
So you won't smell of cheese or of  lamb
stew.

# MY FUNNY OLD TEACHER

She has a nose that sticks out,
Hair in a bun;
And you can't have fun
Except to poke fun at her and her hair.
What would she look like
BARE?
Good God, I'd rather she wore clothes
And then you can't nose
At her underclothes.
She'd have wrinkles,
And I'd rather see crinkles
On her clothes
Than look at her body.
She's got an ugly mole on her neck;
I wonder if it'll get bigger.
But I'd rather see her mole
Than look at her figure.
Wouldn't you?

# FLIPPEN HECK!

Flippen Heck,
Now don't go yet.
Catch that fly before you go.
Catch it, swat it, spray it quick;
Flies and insects make me sick.
They carry dirt and breed disease;
Shoot that one, I beg you please.


Flippen Heck,
Now use a net.
You'll never get him otherwise.
Catch him then and save a life;
Save him trouble death and strife.
Chuck him out the window wide,
Another fly is here inside.
So, Flippen Heck
I won't go yet!!

# PIGS

Pigs will eat anything
You find in a bin.
Soggy corn flakes and
Dried up cakes.
Greasy chips
And apple pips.


They'd eat potato skins
If they're thrown away,
Go for yoghurt
Or curds and whey.
They just do not care
What goes down their throat,
And they gobble and gulp
And often they choke.
Cabbage, and onions, carrots and
swedes,
Pigs always get
Whatever they need.
Their noses go sniffing,
Their snouts in the mud;
Out comes the bucket and
Down with a thud.
The food and the drink
As well as the pulp,
Is scooped up by mouths
In several big gulps.

So if you don't want it,
Remember pigs will.
Leftovers today are
Tomorrow's Pigswill!!!

# KANGAROOS AND SHOES

Kangaroos they don't wear shoes.
They hop, hop, hop,
And never stop.
They carry joey's in their pouches.
The babies bump,
And mothers jump,
Over harsh and rough terrain.
On through desert, on through plain.
Kangaroos they don't need shoes,
Their feet are strong, they travel fast.
Shoes wear out but feet will last
Especially if you are a kangaroo!!

# SELECT A SMELL

The smell of smoke on a cold winter's
night;
The flickering embers of the fading fire
light.
The smell of chicken curry and rice;
Soup in the pan and flavoured with
spice.
The smell of chips or salt from the sea;
Scented seaweed and oil floating free.
The silt dredged up from the bottom of
rivers;
Decomposed fish and pieces of liver.
The smells from the park and muck on
your shoes;
Which of these smells would you
choose?
You might like rubber or chalk or lead,
Coal or wood or flowers instead.
The smell of perfumes or odours or
lotions;
Medicine bottles, various potions.
You might pick tar or turps or paint,
Inhale that lot and you'd feel faint.
So choose one smell or choose a few,
The choice is simply up to you.